Ask Dr K Fisher

about Dinosaurs

Written by
Claire Llewellyn

Illustrated by
Kate Sheppard

KINGFISHER

Claire
(the author)

Kate
(the illustrator)

🐦 KINGFISHER

First published 2007 by Kingfisher
an imprint of Macmillan Children's Books
a division of Macmillan Publishers Ltd
4 Crinan Street London N1 9XW
Basingstoke and Oxford
Associated companies throughout the world
www.panmacmillan.com

Consultant: Dr Phil Manning, Lecturer in Palaentology,
University of Manchester, UK

ISBN 987-0-7534-1455-2

9 8 7 6 5 4 3 2 1
1RD/0908/MPA/SCHOY(MPA)/157MA/C

A CIP catalogue record for this book is available from the British Library.

Printed in China

*For my nephew, Arthur, and for my
friend, Sam. With fondest love – K.S.*

Kingfisher,

Macmillan Children's Books,

4 Crinan Street,

London N1 9XW

www.panmacmillan.com

Ask Dr K Fisher about...

Here's a huge Diplodocus

A weighty problem

Dear Dr K Fisher,
I'm a young female Diplodocus who likes to watch her weight, but just lately it's gone through the roof! I've put on a tonne this year and the smaller, slimmer dinosaurs are laughing at me. Yes, I do eat a lot, but it's all greens and I never touch fast food! What am I doing wrong?

Monumental,
in the meadows

Diplodocus

Ornitholestes

4

Dr K Fisher
Any problem solved!
1 Diving-in-the-Water,
Birdsville KF1 1YZ

Dear **Monumental,**

Don't worry, you are perfectly normal. Diplodocus have a lot of growing to do. When you hatch from your egg, you measure about 1 metre, but as an adult you weigh 40 tonnes and are 36 metres long! You belong to a group of dinosaurs called sauropods – and size is the key to your success. You're too big to be troubled by predators and, towering above the trees as you do, you can feed on leaves that other dinosaurs cannot reach.

Happy eating!

Dr K Fisher

Teething troubles

Tyrannosaurus rex

Edmontosaurus

Triceratops

Dear Dr K Fisher,
I'm a Tyrannosaurus
rex and I have a dental
problem. I'm only young,
but my teeth are dropping
out. I'm meant to be the
scariest hunter on Earth
but I can't frighten
anyone with bare gums.
What's going on?

Toothless Killer,
up the creek

6

Dr K Fisher
Any problem solved!
1 Diving-in-the-Water,
Birdsville KF1 1YZ

Dear **Toothless Killer,**

I can understand your concern. Your teeth are important weapons. Sharp, saw-edged and up to 18 centimetres long, they are great for biting and shaking your prey, and piercing their leathery hides. That's why a few teeth are falling out! But, don't worry, all carnivorous dinosaurs grow new teeth to replace the ones they lose. You will never be without your toothy grin and your useful bite.

Respectfully yours,

Dr K Fisher

Turn the page for **more** on **dinosaur hunters...**

Dr K Fisher's Guide to Dinosaur Hunters

Take a look at these three great dinosaur hunters.

They have everything they need to make a kill – speed, strength, sharp senses, and deadly claws and teeth.

Compsognathus

Height: 50 centimetres
Weight: 3 kilogrammes
Preys on: insects, lizards and mammals
Deadly features:

• Sharp eyes
• Long, narrow jaws with small, sharp teeth
• Three-fingered clawed hands to grip prey
• Long legs for fast running
• Clawed feet to pin down prey

Height: 3 metres
Weight: 60 kilogrammes
Preys on: lizards and small mammals; attacks larger dinosaurs when hunting in a pack
Deadly features:

• Long, strong arms to seize prey
• Grasping hands and large, sharp claws
• Powerful legs for running and jumping
• Huge claw on second toe springs out like a grappling hook so predator can climb up the body of its prey

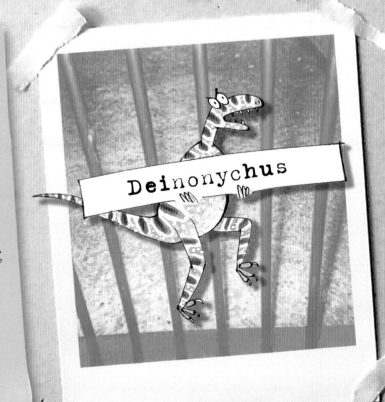

Deinonychus

Height: 12 metres
Weight: 3 tonnes
Preys on: medium and large plant-eating dinosaurs, such as Diplodocus
Deadly features:
• Large, powerful body is fast and agile
• Massive, gaping jaws deliver killer blows
• Long, sharp, saw-edged teeth tear at prey
• Strong arms with hook-like talons grasp prey
• Three strong toes with sharp claws

Allosaurus

Dr K Fisher's Top Tips

 DO steal food from smaller dinosaurs. Eating meat somebody else has caught saves lots of energy. And it's OK to scavenge, too.

 DO stay out of sight when you're shadowing a herd. If the animals see you, they will bunch together and be harder to attack.

 DON'T choose prey that looks strong and healthy. Always try to pick off an animal that is old, or sick or young.

Blowing in the **wind!**

Dear Dr K Fisher,
I'm a Plateosaurus, and I have
an embarrassing problem: wind.
It's painful, it's noisy and (to be honest)
it doesn't smell so nice. I'm afraid I'm
going to lose my friends in the herd.
Is there anything I can do?

Red Faced,
among the ferns

horsetail plants

cycad plants

Plateosaurus

Dr K Fisher
Any problem solved!
1 Diving-in-the-Water,
Birdsville KF1 1YZ

Dear Red Faced,

I'm afraid the culprit is your diet. You eat a lot of cycads, horsetails and Araucaria leaves – tough food that's hard for your body to digest. To help it, you plant-eaters swallow stones, which sit in the gizzard (stomach number 1) grinding the food into softer stuff. When stomach number 2 has also worked on it, your food passes into your gut, where it ferments and gives off gas. Your friends in the herd share this problem. It's best not to be too sensitive about things you cannot change.

Best wishes,

Dr K Fisher

Araucaria tree

Butting in

Dear Dr K Fisher,

I am a Pachycephalosaurus mum and I'm worried about my son. He's always been such a nice boy, but recently he's taken to head-butting other males in the herd. I'm worried he's going to hurt himself and get into terrible trouble. What could have brought this behaviour on, and is there anything I can do to stop it?

Don't Like Trouble, in the herd

Pachycephalosaurus

(males)

Dr K Fisher
Any problem solved!
1 Diving-in-the-Water,
Birdsville KF1 1YZ

Dear **Don't Like Trouble,**
It sounds as if your son has reached the age when he's fighting over girls. In your species this is normal behaviour. The males run and clash heads with one another just like battering rams. It's their way of finding the strongest male to date the females and father the young. Don't worry about him hurting himself: his head is made of almost solid bone so his brain is well-protected.

Kind regards,

Dr K Fisher

Turn the page for **more** on **dinosaur dating...**

13

Dr K Fisher's Guide to Dinosaur Dating

How does a **male dinosaur beat the** other boys and get a date? **What is it that makes them so special?** Meet some successful dinosaur daters, and **find out how to win a female's heart.**

 ## Tyrannosaurus rex

All T-rex live alone and girls are thin on the ground. If I hear one calling for a mate, I make a quick kill and offer her the carcass while it's fresh and juicy. Tempted?

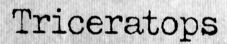

T-rex... loves dining out

Triceratops

Will you take a look at my horns? Aren't they the longest and sharpest? I lock horns with rivals in the herd until they cry for mercy.

Triceratops... he's a sharp guy

14

Protoceratops

I have a large neck frill and a big, attractive bump on my nose. The bump comes in handy as a mean weapon to butt other boys out of the way!

Protoceratops... has all the frills

Dilophosaurus

I've been blessed with a large, bony crest on the top of my head. When I bob my head up and down, the guys see the size of it and they leave the girls to me.

Dilophosaurus... ahead of the rest

Dr K Fisher's Top Tips

DO whatever you can to threaten your rivals: bellow loudly, swing your tail, flash your horns and raise your plates.

DON'T always fight the first male you see. Take your time and look around. Try to pick on someone smaller than you.

DO back down if you're less threatening than your opponent. Only fight if you know you can win.

15

Here's a cooped-up Maiasaura

Give me space!

Dear Dr K Fisher,
I'm a female Maiasaura raising my first family. I'd hoped to bring up my little darlings in a place I could call my own, but I find myself in a huge nest colony packed with hundreds of other mums. It's so crowded I'm at the end of my tether. Does it have to be this way?

Melancholy, in the colony

...Dr. K. Fisher,
1 Diving-in-the-Water,
...Birdsville,
KF1 1Yz

THE COLONY POST

DO NOT DISTURB

Maiasaura colony

16

Dr K Fisher
Any problem solved!
1 Diving-in-the-Water,
Birdsville KF1 1YZ

Dear **Melancholy,**

Raising your young in a colony is a great way to protect them from danger. Maiasaura know there is safety in numbers. While you are finding food for your young, your neighbours protect them from predators on the prowl. Your stay in the colony won't last long. Your hatchlings will soon be strong enough to leave the nest and live on the plains. Next year, you will nest in the colony again. By then it will feel like a home from home and your neighbours will be good friends.

Good luck!

Dr K Fisher

WELCOME

Turn the page for **more** on nesting...

Dr K Fisher's Guide to Nesting

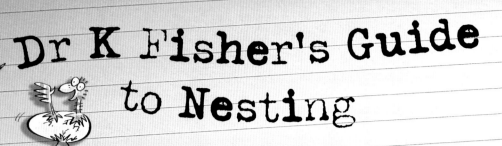

Other dinosaurs nest in colonies, too. One of them, an Oviraptor, has sent me her family album to explain how she builds her nest and how her young ones grow.

Here's yours truly building the nest. I make sure the rim is nice and high to stop my eggs rolling out.

You wouldn't know it from this photo, but I've just laid 24 beautiful eggs! I'm sitting on the eggs to keep them warm.

Number-One-Hatchling smashes through the shell! Her brothers and sisters are just behind.

Three more bundles of trouble: my strong, little hatchlings leave the nest, ready for their first meal.

Dr K Fisher's Top Tips

 DO lay your eggs in neat circles or spirals. Give each egg plenty of space, so your babies have room to hatch.

 DON'T feel you have to copy the Oviraptor. Instead of sitting on your eggs, cover them with a warm layer of plants or soil.

 DON'T worry about the shape of your eggs. Dinosaur eggs can be round, oval or sausage-shaped.

Here's a Eustreptospondylus that wants a swim

What's lurking?

Dear Dr K Fisher,
I am a young Eustreptospondylus.
My mum often takes me to the
seaside to feed along the shore.
Sometimes I want to go in the
water, but my mum won't let me.
She says it's dangerous and I
must wait until I'm bigger. Is she
right or is she just being mean?

Browned Off,
on the beach

Eustreptospondylus

(mum)

Dr K Fisher
Any problem solved!
1 Diving-in-the-Water,
Birdsville KF1 1YZ

Dear **Browned Off**,

Your mum is right. The oceans are packed with deadly sharks, crocodiles and giant marine reptiles. There are also ammonites and jellyfish with nasty nips and stings. You predatory dinosaurs are pretty good swimmers – your bones are light, your legs are strong, and your feet make reasonable flippers – but you could get into difficulties in the currents. It makes sense while you are growing up to stay safe and sound on the shore.

Take care,

Dr K Fisher

Liopleurodon

Cryptocleidus

Here's a Utahraptor that longs to fly

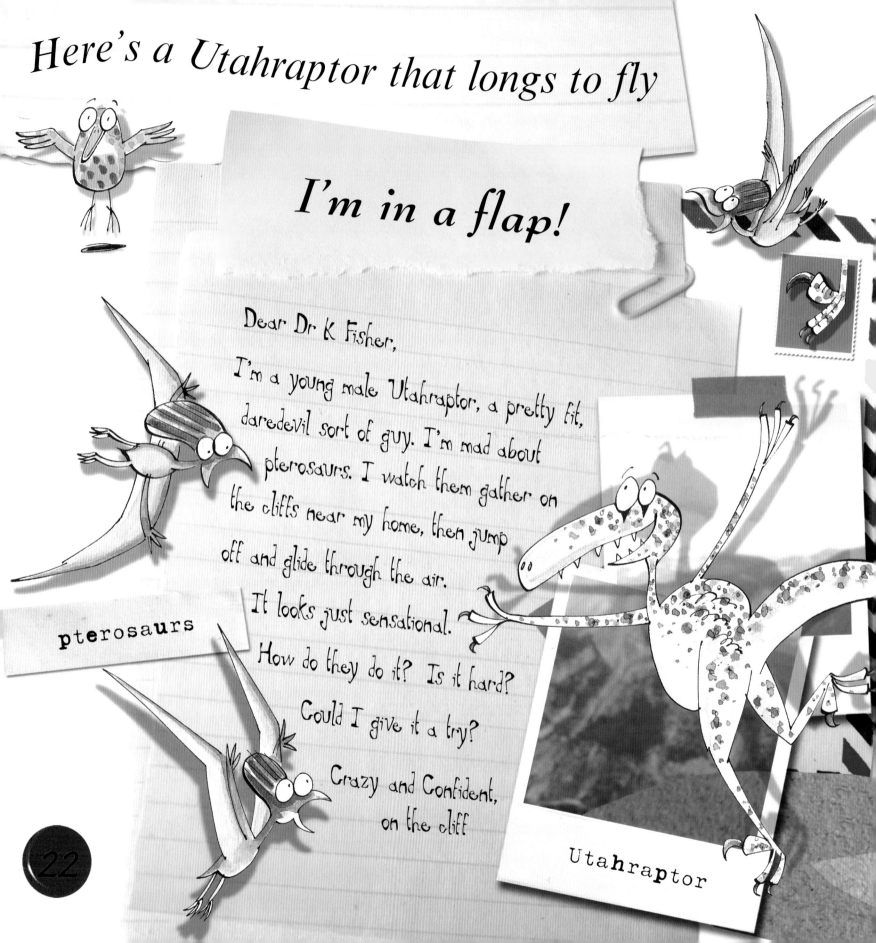

I'm in a flap!

Dear Dr K Fisher,

I'm a young male Utahraptor, a pretty fit, daredevil sort of guy. I'm mad about pterosaurs. I watch them gather on the cliffs near my home, then jump off and glide through the air.
It looks just sensational.
How do they do it? Is it hard?
Could I give it a try?
Crazy and Confident,
on the cliff

pterosaurs

Utahraptor

22

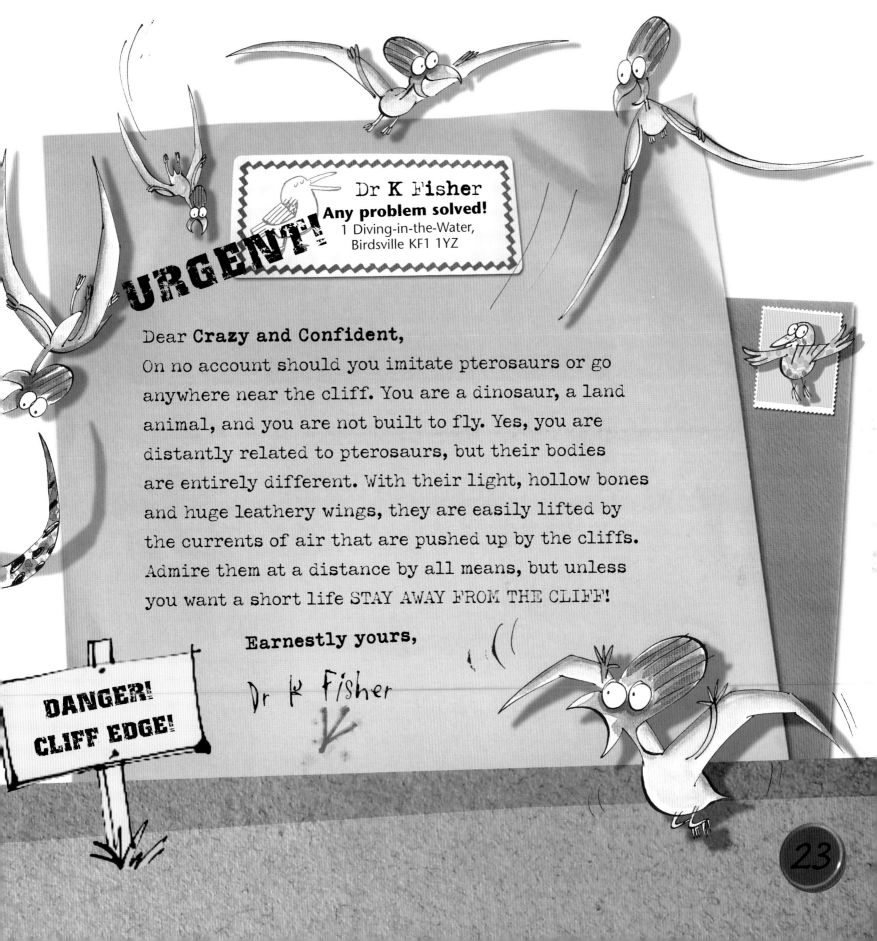

URGENT!

Dear **Crazy and Confident,**

On no account should you imitate pterosaurs or go anywhere near the cliff. You are a dinosaur, a land animal, and you are not built to fly. Yes, you are distantly related to pterosaurs, but their bodies are entirely different. With their light, hollow bones and huge leathery wings, they are easily lifted by the currents of air that are pushed up by the cliffs. Admire them at a distance by all means, but unless you want a short life STAY AWAY FROM THE CLIFF!

Earnestly yours,

Dr K Fisher

DANGER!
CLIFF EDGE!

23

A tale of woe

Dear Dr K Fisher,

I'm a female Euoplocephalus and I'm happy with my body except for one thing — a huge bony lump at the end of my tail. I hate it! It's heavy, unsightly and keeps getting in the way. What is it doing there? Would you advise surgery?

Don't Want To
Be a Freak,
in the forest

Maiasaura

Triceratops

Euoplocephalus

Dr K Fisher
Any problem solved!
1 Diving-in-the-Water,
Birdsville KF1 1YZ

Dear **Don't Want To Be a Freak,**

Your bony lump is called a tail club and it's a great form of defence. When you swing your tail from side to side, you can smash the shins of the largest predators into smithereens. I know you have other protection - your body is covered in hard bony plates - but I would still advise against removing the club. You must keep all your defences intact, particularly as you lead a solitary life without the protection of a herd.

Best wishes,

Dr K Fisher

Albertosaurus
(predator)

Turn the page for **more** on **dinosaur defences...**

25

Dr K Fisher's Guide to Dinosaur Defences

Carnivorous dinosaurs are fast and fierce so what's the best way for prey animals to avoid being eaten? Four defence experts share their experiences.

Ankylosaurus

I'm like an armoured tank. I have bony lumps and plates inside my skin. Try to take a bite out of me and you'll get a mouthful of broken teeth!

Stegosaurus

I have sharp spikes on the end of my tail. One good swing sends the heftiest hunter crashing to the ground.

Triceratops

I weigh five tonnes and have three sharp horns. When I charge at carnivores, I'm unstoppable!

Diplodocus

I'm too big for most predators. If one tries to attack, I lash them and whip them with my tail.

Dr K Fisher's Top Tips

★ DO keep your eyes and ears open. Never be ashamed to run away at the first sign of danger – it's the best defence there is!

★ DO crouch down if a predator comes near. It will help to protect your soft belly from slashing and biting.

★ DON'T forget to use thumb spikes, horns and any other weapons. You may be a herbivore but you can still be aggressive!

27

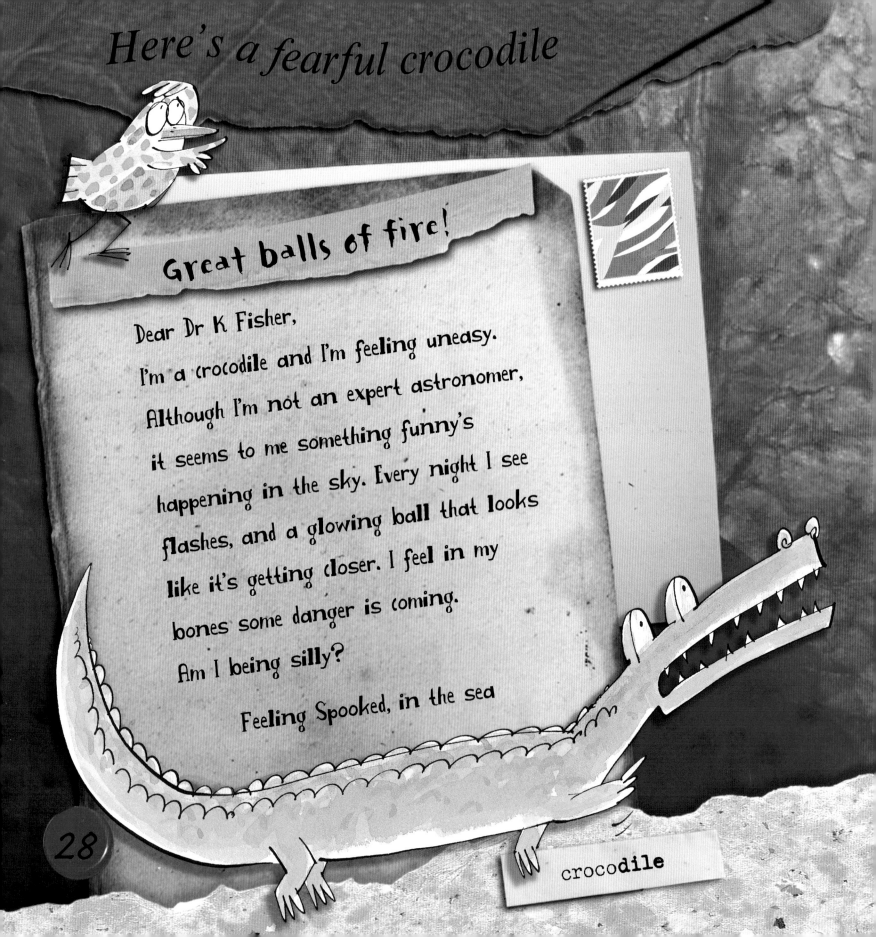

Here's a fearful crocodile

Great balls of fire!

Dear Dr K Fisher,

I'm a crocodile and I'm feeling uneasy.
Although I'm not an expert astronomer,
it seems to me something funny's
happening in the sky. Every night I see
flashes, and a glowing ball that looks
like it's getting closer. I feel in my
bones some danger is coming.
Am I being silly?

Feeling Spooked, in the sea

28

crocodile

Dr K Fisher
Any problem solved!
1 Diving-in-the-Water,
Birdsville KF1 1YZ

Dear **Feeling Spooked**,

Crocodiles, like dinosaurs, have been around for over 165 million years. You are two of the greatest successes of life on Earth. It's true that on our planet species sometimes become extinct. There's a number of reasons for this: meteors or comets crashing into Earth, massive volcanic eruptions, or huge changes in the climate or sea levels. And yet, even in the biggest extinctions, some species manage to survive for the future. I've a feeling you're going to be one of those!

Good luck!

Dr K Fisher

meteor

Edmontosaurus

Pachycephalosaurus

Triceratops

Tyrannosaurus rex

29

Glossary

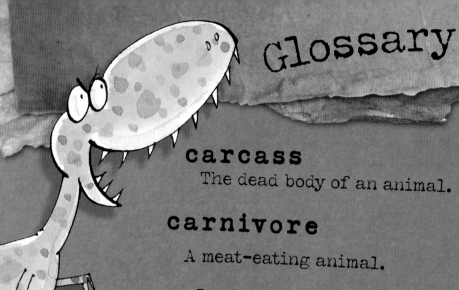

carcass

The dead body of an animal.

carnivore

A meat-eating animal.

colony

A group of animals that live closely together.

comet

A cloud of frozen gases, ice and dust that goes around the sun.

current

Air or water that flows in a particular direction.

eruption

When a volcano shoots out gas, ash and red-hot rock.

extinct

No longer living on Earth.

ferments

Breaks down, changes and gives off gas.

gizzard

An extra stomach in some animals that is used to grind tough food.

hide

The skin of an animal.

meteors

Lumps of rock from space that crash into the Earth.

predators

Animals that hunt other animals for food.

prey

Animals that are hunted and eaten by other animals.

pterosaurs

A group of flying reptiles that lived in the dinosaur age.

talons

Sharp, hooked claws.

Guide to Dinosaur Names

Dinosaurs have long Latin names that are hard to say. Find out what they mean and how to pronounce them by using this handy guide.

Albertosaurus (al-bert-oh-saw-russ) – means 'Alberta lizard'
Allosaurus (al-oh-saw-russ) – means 'other lizard'
Ankylosaurus (an-kie-loh-saw-russ) – means 'stiff lizard'
Compsognathus (komp-sog-nath-us) – means 'elegant jaw'
Deinonychus (die-non-i-kuss) – means 'terrible claw'
Dilophosaurus (die-loaf-oh-saw-russ) – means 'two-ridge lizard'
Diplodocus (di-plod-oh-kuss) – means 'double beam'
Edmontosaurus (ed-mon-toe-saw-russ) – means 'Edmonton lizard'
Euoplocephalus (you-oh-plo-kef-ah-lus) – means 'well-armoured head'
Eustreptospondylus (ewe-strep-toe-spon-die-luss) – means 'well-curved vertebra'
Maiasaura (my-ah-saw-rah) – means 'good mother lizard'
Ornitholestes (or-nith-oh-les-teez) – means 'bird robber'
Oviraptor (oh-vee-rap-tor) – means 'egg thief'
Pachycephalosaurus (pack-i-kef-al-oh-saw-russ) – means 'thick-headed lizard'
Plateosaurus (plat-ee-oh-saw-russ) – means 'first lizard'
Protoceratops (pro-toe-ker-ah-tops) – means 'first horned face'
Stegosaurus (steg-oh-saw-russ) – means 'roof lizard'
Triceratops (tri-serra-tops) – means 'three-horned face'
Tyrannosaurus rex (tie-ran-oh-saw-russ rex) – means 'tyrant lizard'
Utahraptor (yoo-tah-rap-tor) – means 'Utah plunderer'

Flying reptiles:
pterosaurs (terr-oh-saws) – means 'winged lizards'

Marine reptiles:
Cryptocleidus (crip-toe-clide-us) – means 'hidden collar-bone'
Liopleurodon (li-ploo-ra-don) – means 'smooth-sided tooth'

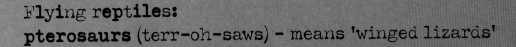

Index